The Relatable Poetry Journal

NICOLE ROSE JULIAN

ARCHWAY
PUBLISHING

Archway Publishing books may be ordered through booksellers or by contacting:

Archway Publishing
1663 Liberty Drive
Bloomington, IN 47403
www.archwaypublishing.com
844-669-3957

ISBN: 978-1-6657-4488-1 (sc)
ISBN: 978-1-6657-4489-8 (e)

Print information available on the last page.

Archway Publishing rev. date: 06/14/2023

To those who never heard the right words when they needed to hear them, or couldn't find the words to say because they feared them.
You are not alone.
You are enough.

❤ The Relatable ❤
Poetry Journal

Nicole Rose Julian

Foreword by Casey Suddeth

Art by
Tiffany Daniel – Jones
Vince Elra
Madi
Nicole Rose Julian

Contents

Foreword

Everyone has that friend who makes them say to themselves, "I wish I were as good as them." At least I hope you do, so you feel as lucky as I do. Nicole is that very friend. They make you want to do better. He inspires you to get off your feet and do something about something. She is a true friend to the core.

The Relatable Poetry Journal is just that: relatable. Nicole's words will constantly have you thinking, *I feel that* in a modern way. Their voice makes you feel understood, and even in the parts where you maybe feel you can't relate, Nicole's voice makes it happen anyway. Too bad.

If only I knew the friendship that awaited me when auditioning for Nicole's project in college. The beautiful friendship immediately persevered through the trial of fire; we arrived in each other's lives at a crucial axis point. It is a foundation of trust I treasure to this day. We both had some growing to do, but we managed to do it.

We all love a good page-turner, a new chapter, in stories, in life. *The Relatable Poetry Journal* boldly states the turning of a page. Yet only after reflecting on the notes of pages and chapters that precede it, do you begin to understand, every precious scribble in the margins of life closely annotated and analyzed, until it is scribbled out, marked through, highlighted, or gleefully burned with every emotion.

Everything good, bad, hurtful, inspiring, and everything in between has been mentally noted and spilled out before the pages to be seen and heard. Every stubbed toe, every long shift, every ignored glance is taken into account and followed with that simple, relatable question: "Right?"

We all want to take that train to having our thoughts permanently transposed by ink or graphite, but Nicole actually bought a ticket. This journal is a first step taken, but with a hand dangling behind for you to grab onto and pull you along, without a shred of hesitation. I hope you link hands with Nicole and take a step forward. As they display the path taken for self-realization and confidence, I hope you follow that relatable voice echoing in these pages.

That beautiful, bold, black, queer, non-binary, relatable voice fills me with immense pride. Congratulations! You've finished the foreword that might as well be spelled "forward," just as Nicole's voice moves forward. Now turn that literal and metaphorical page, you beautiful person.

—Casey Suddeth
Actor, writer, and friend

Chapter 1

Life

I have a gift with words.
They surge from my brain from time to time.
I have this sublime sensation to write
my own combination of those twenty-six letters.

But lately
it's been hard.

The land my writing comes from is scarred,
struck repeatedly by the lightning of chaos
and all things outside of my control.
Uncertainty stole all my thoughts
and feelings of control.
But I continue to stroll through
the world as it goes up in flames.

I feel so lame.
All I have is words.

No skills to help the mills
keep running.
But my words unwritten
turn into thoughts.
Plots lingering like children
waiting to be picked for kickball.
A free-for-all for all who see the light of day,
this poem fought hard to be here today.

So I acquiesced.
Ideas become obsessed with the hope of outside validation,
that divine sensation to feel important.
So these are my words.
I hope they help you as much as they've helped me.

-Words

I'm on a hero's journey.
The only things I see are behind and one step in front of me.
My call to adventure was the sun rising and my venture out of bed.
My head is aching from the trials and failures of the past,
as I hope for my growth to last and
the new skills I've acquired be helpful.
I died and was reborn and swore an oath
to change the world with my revelations.
I wish to give people the sensation of belonging and love and show the beauty this
world is really made of,

so when I return home, I'll know my hero's journey was worth it.
-Hero's Journey

Gotta go to work—no time to twerk the night away,
as if I have the muscles to do it.
Work through it; you can do it.

Gotta go to work—
that keeps the lights on.
Got it goin' on, and gotta keep it that way.
Can't let that style sway
as I sashay through life,
avoiding the spike
and staying on point.
My thoughts and joints
wiggle and squeak
just enough to disturb the peace
and make the week's top-ten list.
Listen, please—I insist as I persist
with my rhyming and excellent timing
as I try to make bank at my day job.

HELLO
my name is

Nicole
not so happy to help you

Gotta go to work
where they play that one song
all day long
that I can't stand.
I stand in hostess land
that sadly doesn't have cupcakes.
Some birthday cakes leave me with toothaches
with how sweet they are.
I plan to go far, far away from here
and play and go on adventures.
Venture where few women have gone.
Following my destiny on—to write in spite of those who say I can't.

So I will continue to stand in hostess land with no cake, making small bank as I
prep to make the world quake with my words.
I'll yell my stories from the rooftops if they will make someone's day.
But there is an easier way, and it requires funds.
And that's why I gotta go to work.
-Gotta Go to Work

I have been thrown off balance
by the winds of challenge for not facing my own fears.
Tears seem to endlessly flow down my face
from the things I can't seem to face.
Things I couldn't ever imagine taking place
are now things I face every day,
and all old fears are amplified.
I hate to admit I'm terrified.
I'm not qualified to deal with such things.
I was taught to sing and dance,
not deal with happenstance of people
in power's choices
and the sadness and chaos in my loved ones' voices.
I am underqualified to deal with such things,
but there is no one else to clean up these broken things.
So the job must be mine.
My heart is kind.
My love is colorblind.
-Balance

Oh!

Look at that!

Life just threw a wrench in the machine of your life.

Your gears grind as you scramble and stress over why this happened to you,

upset you,

and made you sad too.

But look at that—you learned something new:

that your life machine can handle more than you knew,

so when it happens again, you'll better understand how to mend it,

because it will happen again.

You'll just be ready then.

Explore it, deplore it, but you can't ignore it.

We are not in control of all the things that happen to us.

But with faith, trust, and a little love from the rest of us, we can get through anything,

together.

-*We are Not in Control*

The future will always be uncertain.
It all can rearrange in the blink of an eye.
With just one choice,
everything can change.
I fear something's wrong in my brain.
My frame of mind is a little broken.
My heart and mind haven't spoken in some time.

I may unwind at this rate,
with the state of things outside.

Where is my mind?

Everything has changed.
I know I'm not the same.
My heart has spoken and agreed
to keep beating as long as
I keep seeking better change,
to keep my brain from moving
too fast so my calm moments can last.
Forget the past and remember that change is good.
-*Everything Can Change*

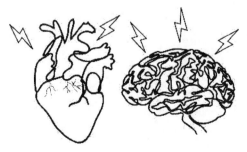

You have the might to be great.
Do great things—be amazing.
Hesitating?
Are we?
Then maybe your dreams are just big enough.
It's the tough ones who have said if they don't scare you,
you must dream *bigger*!
What's your dream trigger?
A nice song, a long jog, or maybe early morning fog?
Cold air against your cheek,
the sound of raindrops as they drip off the window seal,
that feeling you get after seeing a good movie,
or maybe watching people as you sip your smoothie?
Sometimes you can feel loony with how simple the trigger can be
For you to say, "That sounds like me."
The way the sun leaks through your fingers is different than mine.
You're the one who can explain it best.
You're not like all the rest.
You don't have to be the best, but you could be.
So, you see, all it takes is that one step
to believe in the dream and dare to go bigger.
Use your dream trigger in the most creative way and do not sway toward doubt.
No doubt. Go get some clout.
Rock out! Stand out! 'Cause there is no doubt.
You could be great. You just have to believe it.
-You Could be Great

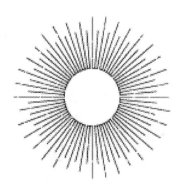

A Series of Unfortunate Nights #1

I'm not OK. My brain is out of frame. The picture has a fixture out above it, and I can't find a replacement bulb. I am the hub of distress at the moment, and my head wants to explode. I feel like I'm about to implode. Overload of unhappy thoughts—the fairy dust won't work for me, Peter. I can't fly. I sigh. I can barely walk. The weight of my unbearable fate is crushing me. I might not be anything. Continuing to be nothing to the world but another millennial forced to just exist. A mist in the night of an ever-cold October night where I am filled to the brim with sadness without a reasoning behind it. Just unhappy with her circumstances. I could write stanzas about that, but mainly I am just plain unhappy. Nothing sappy—I'm just fucking unhappy. And I don't know what to do about it. I have tried everything. Booze, pressing snooze, sex, and diving into another. I did things I can't tell my mother. But nothing. I'm tired but can't sleep. I weep often.

-Something is coming—
something good.
The agreement is understood.
I did all I could.
I would ask the sky when this something will be here,
but the universe keeps me sincere.
When is still unclear.
But something is near.
I can feel it.

The eye jumps.
I cringe.
The worry wins as it bends me backward
with sadness and stress.
A mass of unrest with no sign of sleep.
Not a peep in days.
Days seem to blend together as the weather gets no better.
It seems to only rain—
something I usually like,
but in the city, it just adds strife
to everything.
Sadly, this rain is a pain
that has added a strain on my brain
that won't go away.
Am I insane?
Is this what insanity feels like?

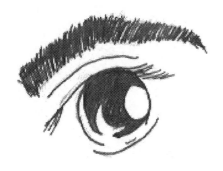

The eye jumps.
My mind erupts
with all of my past failures,
sailing years away in my brain.
Things that normal people refrain
from talking about—
the things that make them sad and mad and
uncertain of how to make it better.
My eye jumps once again.

When will this end?
Is it the lights?
I don't know.
I don't think I can bend any farther.
Every day seems to get harder.
I can't wait.
This pain won't dissipate.
This is what I hate.
Feeling helpless.
I need sleep.
My eye jumps again.
-The Jumping Eye

I'm feeling wired, with my eyes strained and drained of all pep.
Earlier I could do happy reps and take bets with how far I would go
with all the energy I had.
Now everything is a drag.
My mind has a lag and things are fuzzy, woozy, woo—
went out for a sec.
I really hope this doesn't last,
that my journey to my bed is fast
because I'm tired of being tired.
-*Being Tired*

I was afraid I forgot how to write
because of how much I type.
But to lose my ability to handwrite, a novel, a poem, a letter of love, and
so on.

To lose my voice without a keyboard,
not be heard,
I know it's absurd, but is it?
'Cause if we quit it handwriting altogether,

we may lose it.
Confuse it with chicken scratch, detach and lose our connections,
our obsessions, confessions, and life lessons,

Lost

without a keyboard or something to click on.
We live on the written word so we can all be heard.
I will trade my computer to feel smoother with a pen in hand...

'Cause man...
I don't want to feel that way again.
So I'll just sit here with my pen and remember how to write.
-Handwriting

I work nights.
With the hum drum of everyday life,
a dumb dumb like me
likes to work at night.
There is something about night,
the world without daylight.
It's truly a sight.
So to my delight, I work at night.

Night lights—
they glow instead of burn.
You yearn for their warmth.
Grab a cup of tea;
that works
to do a good night's work.
Light a candle
to set the mood;
fine tune the music
to light background noise.
Just tools and hacks for
a good night's work.
Now sit...breathe.
What do you see?

Please do tell me.
For the night work that gets done is unsung. I love to discuss what others have done.
See 'cause night work is a niche—
an itch that not all scratch; not all are willing to snatch up the time to do good, night
work.
So I work nights, so the next time I see daylight, something new will remain.
-Night Work

How does one time coffee?
So free once it's had, but so sad and sleepy when it's not.
I like mine hot in the form of tea.

The only person I'm fooling is me,
for my need for caffeine is real.
Surreal how bad I need the feel of caffeine running through my veins.

But oh the pains of choosing when to have it!
To start things off with a bang?
Or
use it as my last minute nitro to blow through the rest of the day?

Hmmm, the really difficult question...
when will the coffee be ready?
-*Coffee Time*

Why is it that I can always have time to be there for others—
my sister, mother, significant other—
but when I need someone,
I can never get a hold of anyone.
Sometimes it's a bad time.
Sorry the timing of my meltdown
was not divine.
I just need someone on the line—
someone who loves me.
But this feeling inside of me
I just can't shake.
This ache—
my broken heart lies and waits.
You should really talk to someone.
But none will understand,
and if they did?
Why burden someone else with these...
illogical feelings?
I am loved.
I'm not alone.
But these feelings have formed like stone,
that I can't crack.
Even in a life with no lack,
I feel...trapped.
I love you.
The last thing I wanna do is be a burden.
-Burden

A Series of Unfortunate Nights #4

I am waiting in the dream waiting room. I sit as the lights buzz and flicker from forever staying on—and on and on and on. My friends have all gone in. They clearly heard their names called once their opportunity came, where I feel mine has gone up in flames but no one bothered to tell me. How many stories must I desperately make only to be turned down? To constantly feel so close yet so far away. My heart seams are starting to fray and I don't know how to fix it. I'm running out of thread to keep sewing it up. I'm afraid to dream up something else, 'cause I might get my hopes up...but if I fall off another cloud I don't think I will make it. My mother is drowning in bills I can't help her pay. What am I really good at anyway? What can I do? Can't even make my own fucking dreams come true? As others' dreams have faded and died, mine still lives...right? Or did I just miss the telegram? Missed an eye exam where I clearly missed my dream highway off ramp. I don't know. I'm scared. What if I don't make it? What if I can't help her pay it? But what if I don't make it? And I've already missed my appointment? And now I'm just wasting my time...

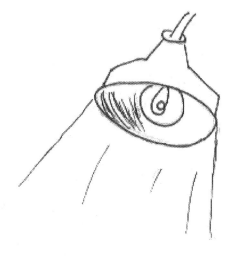

I Miss Being A Teen

Watching football players run up and down the field,
the cheerleaders sing and spiel, spelling words of encouragement.
Kinda wishing you were as fit as they were.

Back when saying hi to the hot guy in history meant everything and adult problems
meant nothing.
To sing in the spring musical,
Passing math was critical, and I was a lot less cynical.

The amount of likes you put in front of someone's name now feels really lame, but
back then you just wanted them to feel the same, so you could kiss in the rain like
all the teen movies...ever!

When summer felt like forever, to not see all your friends.
When fun would never end until Mom called about curfew and it was time to
head out.

Going back would be a cop out.
I love looking at my diploma too much.
Such drama made everything so exciting,
making every moment terrifying yet satisfying.

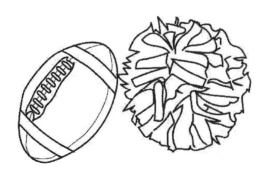

Today I won, but tomorrow I might lose
and choose to succumb to feeling numb again,
to not feel,
to steal precious time and waste it on TV and trashy magazines,
to exist and resist all productivity.
I just wish everything I did mattered,
that not all my thoughts would scatter
the moment I found something brilliant:
precious thoughts, lost, tossed, forgotten.
That's why I keep pens everywhere,
'cause it's unfair to my mind to forget the great things it thinks up.
So I'll be ready when my brain wakes up,
to not fuck up the good stuff that comes my way
and not stray from my destiny
when I have so many things to look forward to, things to do.
So I can't be lazy.
That won't do.
Not doing what I have to do is not being true to myself but also knowing when I need
help.
To be free of all afterthoughts as greatness trots my way.
So my thoughts mustn't sway toward doubt,
making myself feel left out of the success party.
So let's start.
Leave the pity party and not feel sorry for not being the very best,
yet.
But I bet your great moment is right around the corner.
So I will be the best I can be today.
Lay in bed and be content—I mean grateful—
that I'm not bent over in pain,
going insane,
allowed to feel a little lame, but know
I'm not off my game for keeping my routine the same.
I'm where I'm supposed to be today,
a little cray but that's okay.
I'm only human.
-Human

I've been running most of my life.
Run, don't walk to your destinations.
All work relations require time and time is money, honey.
So I became okay with running.

Running the rat race
at a pace that had me going nowhere.
fast.

Who can last like this?
In a system built on the backs of the hard working class,
it's not built to last.

I wanna make a class of my own
where I can afford a home all on my own,
feel grown,
so the only place I have to run to is
home.
-Running

A car crash,
day ruined—
metals smashing into one another,
never knowing each would meet this way.
Stay in your lane, they say, but not everyone does.
You must judge with your own eyes
the size

and the distance between you and another car's existence with such a persistence
your brain can get tired.
Drink your coffee—
now you're wired.
Great.
Stand still traffic—
It's tragic really.

If I just squeeze past—
that was my last thought
before I crashed.
You could be dashed,
slashed,
completely extinguished
in a second.
You have the time to wait
for the light.
Trust me.
-Car Crashing

A shock—
one small nick or scrap and your heart drops.
I have to stop and think.
Why do I suddenly feel like I need sleep?
I can't keep this inside, yet I wanna hide.
Find someone to speak to,
release to,
who can help me break free too.
Maybe you?
No, no not you.
Another person to feel like a burden to.
But I have to do something, right?
I can't see an end in sight.
I wanna fight and scream.
I feel like an athlete without a team
Everyone is there, except in my time of need.
I need a break
so I can shake off this feeling of ache
like dead skin—
find myself again.
No booze or weed—
I just need to breathe.
-Shock-

Apply, apply, apply, they say.
An entry-level position is the way.
You need two to three years of experience by the way—
what?
I thought this was to gain said experience?
Uh...was there something that I missed?
I insist
I can do this job; it's no prob.
I don't want this job but I'll take it,
because the money will help me make it,
to just barely survive.
You ask if I have a BS to answer your phones
alone.
Just answering your phone
now requires four years of study.
I couldn't afford that, honey.
So now you won't let me make money.
That's BS. To assess someone before
they've done anything
is a sure way to leave a position open.
The worker's paradox is to get someone new
but not new
so you don't have to train them
or pay them their worth.
So henceforth the gap
between
upper and middle class   widens.
The poor get poorer
and the rich get richer.
God bless America.
-Work Paradox

No work got done today.
The moment I wished to start my thoughts swayed
to the beating and throb behind and just above my eyes.
Sighs...
Advil, please be my ally.
Two liquid gels down the hatch.
Ah,
that's the catch to not drinking enough water,
or
did I wander for too long and forget to eat?
My brain feels like it needs sleep,
where rest and quiet meet.
But I don't have time to sleep...
Throb
Throb
Okay—I'll close my eyes for ten minutes.
Mad brain wins as I wince at light like a vampire.
I close my eyes and the knot in my head unwinds,
no longer confined to four walls as my brain stretches and yawns.
My thoughts wander about what I have to do with my day;
they slowly slip away as I float in the atmosphere,
like floating in a pool at the perfect temp.
I don't know where the throb went.
My phone chimes,
I open my eyes;
The throb is gone as I move on with my day.
-Headache

You did it.

You won.

You mean me?

You have the wrong someone.

You're impressed with something *I've* done?

What is this?

A joke?

A poke to my side just to get a reaction?

But there is a fraction of hope—

nope. *Nope.*

We're not supposed to hope, 'cause it puts us in a place that's hard to cope when we *fail.*

The loss hits like a *big* bag of rocks—

no stocks in hope.

But here you are telling me I'm dope.

Not a common trope or cliché

but to say my words slay and made you feel something.

That's something I *hoped* for.

What is this?

Recognition?

Is self-validation a condition?

In my mission to get a point across and clear my thoughts,

you're saying you understood?

And liked it?

Now that's something.

-What Is This?

I got upset today over something I can't control.

It's both sad and funny.

It was over money.

Working a job that will rob me of precious living time,

my XP will lower significantly working a nine to five or even part time.

To work, just to stay afloat on a boat that is sinking.

To work in a sinking ship of a system that isn't catered to an artist's way of thinking.

I refuse to get on that boat—for as long as I can cope without it.

I just want to write.

It feels like my birthright in a country famed for its "freedoms."

Unfortunately *freedom* is colorblind and mainly sees in shades of white.

But I don't have too much spite.

I just wanna write. It just feels right.

I wanna help improve someone's sight in this world,

put things into perspective

like an artistic detective with a rhyming habit.

I just want to write,

not fight but spread love.

A connoisseur of inspiration, liberation, and maybe the sensation of feeling less alone.

Being kind is something I can control,

so enjoy.

-I Just Want to Write

I never saw it coming at all,

my fall,

my descent from grace.

I don't know where I went.

Deadlines came and went.

My energy, always spent,

just this constant lethargy

and feelings of being trapped.

My system's hacked,

hijacked

by a stranger who wears my face.

Loved ones say I should clean myself up,

Dress up, and go out somewhere,

but where?

Going out won't get my work done.

This battle with myself seems like it can't be won.

Excuses, excuses, excuses—

I'm tired.

I feel wired.

Maybe I need a break.

I feel useless in this weak state.

Today my mild depression, said checkmate.

But if growing up has showed me anything,

This too shall pass.

This won't last forever.

Let's charge our mental batteries so when we do feel up to things, there will be no need for excuses.

Things will simply get done.

-*Excuses*

Timing,
strategizing,
realizing I need to find something
to come up with to say,
"Hey!"
With time is something
you can't play.
It's not just a thing;
it's a living entity that
grows and shrinks.
It builds
and tears things apart.

Timing,
climbing,
finding that time
will never stop
for me; we and no one
being can take it from
its throne.
It owns us
because we can't get enough
of its funds,
'cause time is rich
and so easily spent
on things and people we think matter.
-Timing

What is a choice?

Is it just a sound I make with my voice or in my head?

No.

It's a decision.

What's a decision?

A list made with precision about all the reasons to do something.

Something. Something.

That's a lot of things that lead to another something.

But some things are harder to break down than that.

How do I get all the facts?

Truth is...

you can't.

There isn't a plant you can just pick the knowledge from.

It costs more than any lump sum.

Time and trust must be your guide.

Because your list of reasons that grows with each coming season is infinite.

Your list will never finish, but your decision won't wait all day.

You got a choice to make.

-Choice

How to cope—
nope.
No one said that...
yeah...no one.

There is no one scope to look through to answer that question,
thus why I put these words in succession,
so I can be the one to answer this question.
Coping takes many forms,
Can look like moping.
Flat out sadness

is often confused with madness to cover up a reason,
a treason against the state of you.
What do you do?
Who did this to you?

But what if the bad guy...is you?
That left a sty on the eye you use to see straight and show the world.
Then you begin to uncurl, unravel—
how could you have been so stupid to play this raffle?
But you didn't.

Don't even remember buying a ticket,
yet here you are. A game you never asked to be a part of.
You've gotten this far.
Yet you don't know where you are. Lost.

Lost to thoughts,
to sounds—
oh here comes the ground.
You've fallen into the pit again.
You look around.

Look up—a cloud
with a sky so blue you wanna cry.
Then suddenly you feel happy to be alive,
and you notice the stones and cracks in the walls around you
                                        go all the way to the top,
                                            so you climb.
                                               Don't stop,
                            not till you get to the top.
                As you claw your way up, you do stop,
but just to breathe.
The sun gets brighter.
You're much higher than where you were before.
You can feel it.

                        The warmth of happiness on your skin—
                                it's there waiting for you.
                                    Just at the top there.

One last step and you get there.
You stare out into the openness of this vast existence—
not what you expected.
Might as well watch
the sunset.
-*Learning To Cope*

Chapter 2

Love

Sunday mornings is what I want my love to look like.
To wake up to mid- to late-morning light
with the one I love in my sight, as they get out of bed to start our day.
I follow soon after.

Not too long the apartment is filled with laughter.
They made breakfast,
threw the dish towel at the sink. They missed.
Participation kiss, as I list the things I need to do for the week.
Can we go back to sleep?
Couch it is.
This.

It's the Sunday mornings I'm after.
All disasters can wait, 'cause it's Sunday.
The rest of the world can wait till Monday.
'Cause I'm with the one I love on Sunday.
-*Sunday Mornings*

I Like You—Love Poem #1

I like you a lot more than I expected to.
And so soon I'm writing a poem about you.

Wrapped up in a cocoon of all these lovely emotions,
no longer going through the motions, but present.
This is a present, a gift,

a new person to spend time with.
To laugh and cry and possibly chase butterflies, if people still do that.
In fact, that cocoon I spoke of filled with puppy love,

may make me into more of a bird than a butterfly.
But we will just have to wait and see
what becomes of me.
I just know I like you,
and that's enough for me.

-Blue eyes-
Blue skies that seem incapable of lies
fill my mind like a bucket in water—
cool, crisp, blue water.
I melt with your gaze.
You amaze with how bright you are,
how deep you can scar
when your eyes go dark and lose their spark.

How dare the world wreck such a beautiful work of art.
Those baby blues
that shine with glee,
that are so happy to see me—
my body sings and rings with you near.
Your eyes peer into my soul
and I'm not cold,
but warm.

A sweet song for a sweet boy
who's been on my mind first thing when I
wake up
and
right before I sleep.
So I play this one song on repeat
because it reminds me of you,
for you have part of my heart to keep.
So yes—a sweet song for a sweet boy that I
can't wait to meet.
-A Sweet Song

I like to think I found the secret to life early on.
It's not for everyone,
thus why people are constantly searching for
"The One."
But there are five things actually:
French fries,
milkshakes,
movie theater popcorn,
buttered croissants,
and someone to share them with.
-Five Things

The Legend of the Dark Samurai

There once was a dark samurai; he wore all black and had a scar over one eye.
He had seen many battles and many obstacles he did tackle.
Oftentimes he surprised himself with his success,
yet his day to day left him unimpressed.
So the young samurai ventured out, slightly south, toward the coast.

The distance he didn't mind at most.
It was there he met the maiden with purple hair.
She saw a darkness in the samurai's stare.
For her it did not scare but intrigued.

She followed his darkness that not all could see.
The maiden felt pure glee to be with the samurai and his dark eyes,
seeing behind his guise
dark brown eyes.

The feeling of his warm embrace,
the way he tastes on her lips,
his sweet kiss—it just makes sense.
Who knew purple and black could feel as good as this?

I dreamed of the forest
and the man who lingered there.
The cold, crisp air
brushed my cheek and entered my lungs.
The look of the sun as it bleeds through my fingers.
Now the man's touch lingers.
The moss and the trees greet us as if old friends,
as the man and I ascend
into their home—
our home,

where we roam
and feel safe,
away from the harsh
landscape of civilization—
that place that seems
so far away now.
How could I ever
leave this place,
his warm embrace?

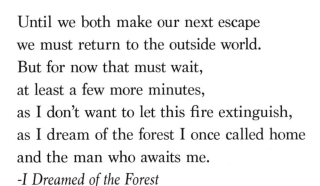

Until we both make our next escape
we must return to the outside world.
But for now that must wait,
at least a few more minutes,
as I don't want to let this fire extinguish,
as I dream of the forest I once called home
and the man who awaits me.
-I Dreamed of the Forest

Dry Eyes—Love Poem #2

When I seem hard to find or like I don't want to speak to you,

that's not true.

I get dry eyes and...
I don't want you to think I cry every time
I see you.
But you're beautiful, so it's understandable.

Dark Samurai Legend Continues

There once was a dark samurai who wore all black and had a scar over one eye. He was accompanied by a maiden whom he cared for deeply. Her hair was purple, soft, and silky. Together, they travelled in search of knowledge to gaze upon and think of after.

The samurai was always on a quest for new things to learn, to discern for himself, sharing how he felt, which made the maiden's heart melt with how happy the samurai felt for just learning something new. For she was also learning, but not just facts and fictions—learning that of the samurai's intentions: to use his knowledge for the invention of a better world for them and all to live in and come to. The samurai's tactics were developing at their fastest along with his skills, and the purple-haired maiden matched it.

Anything they wanted, they could have it. The world they knew began to bend to their will. Sometimes if you're still, you can hear them laughing with knowing so much and nothing all at once, happy with what they knew and ready for whatever came their way.

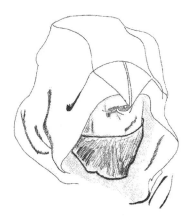

I know this may seem hard to believe, in your current
state of need, wanting, or loss, feeling lost or unseen, like
a book that no one wants to read.
But you must understand that you are still beautiful.

Even as tears stream down your face, I am stunned by
your grace. But how could you know? You only see your
face in mirrors and photographs.
You missed your laugh or
the way you light up looking at stained glass or art,
your energy from your warm heart and kind soul. You
deserve to feel whole.
So I am here to remind you

that you've never seen you the way I see you:
beautiful through-and-through,
especially when you don't feel like it.
That's you in your rawest form—
The best time to be adored.

Please don't cry or sigh or deny me when I tell you that
you are beautiful
'cause you've never seen you like I do.
-You've Never Seen Yourself

Beauty is
in the mind's eye of the beholder,
the holder of the mighty cup
that's filled with the tears
of your peers unable to find beauty
between their own ears and under their noses.
So many poses in the mirror
that just aren't clear as beauty to some.
It's strange.
Beauty isn't glum or unbothered.
But it can be sad,
so sad,
yet also can be the definition of glad, happy, and gay.

I like my beauty sad most days
for without the sadness,
we can't appreciate the good.
That's something nature has understood
since the beginning of time.
When snow falls and trees die,
when rain falls from the sky, it's beautiful.
But the beauty of a smile?
Let's sit with that awhile.
Turn that smile into a laugh.

It's beautiful:
the mad dash just before it rains;
making it to see the show;
getting lost in someone's eyes;
the surprise of good news—
that's beautiful.
But when you can open your eyes
and see yourself in all your glory and say, "I'm beautiful,"
you've made it.

-Beauty

I Forget

I think everyone is beautiful—
even myself, most of the time—
but I often find myself overwhelmed with everyone else's beauty,
so I forget.
So your reminders are welcomed and appreciated.
I'll make sure to remind you as often as I can.

Beautiful Moment #3

Connecting. Sweet. We meet and instantly connect. You are correct that one thing is awesome. I'm happy you agree. I see you. As you do you, someone new who gets you. There are so few cool people like you. What do you do? Yep, still cool. I'm not gonna be a fool. We should be friends. And it's great 'cause I don't have to pretend to like things that I don't like, 'cause you already get it. I'm with it. Let's connect.

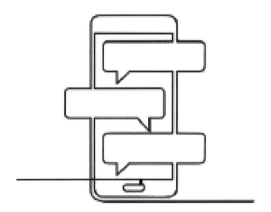

TNF

I tried so hard to make you love me.
All our friends would plead with me to give up on us being a we.
But something in me craved your intimacy, but I was
too young to know what that means.

I confused lust with love.
You shoved me away and I kept coming back.
But you gave me knowledge that I lacked.
So when I packed all my things to go,
I took my broken pride with me.

Not needing to love you
forced me to love myself.
For every idea of you I adored, left me sore,
'cause I had to absorb that you didn't love me—
and you never did.
I'm sorry for myself, for looking to someone else to fix me.
I thought we had something.
I'm not sorry for what you taught me.
I realized what I couldn't see.
We were never meant to be a we.
I hope you found what you need.

I did.

I always considered myself to be a wandering soul
with no console when times got dark.
My heart was broken and cracked
from lack in times of need—
when all I need is just a hug from someone I love,
who I know loves me back and that sense of lack, lessens.

I don't go to church,
but I prayed for these blessings:
to be less lonely in these times of destressings.
But my fear of messing everything up
when you came along
just prolonged the sadness,
'cause I was afraid if I let you into my madness,
you would leave.

It feels like everyone leaves,
but you didn't.
I have to admit it,
you surprised me,
revitalized me,
and stayed—

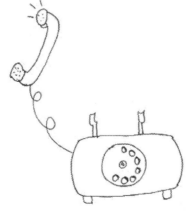

stayed on the phone
when no one else would pick up.
You picked up.
I wondered if it was hiccup,
a stick up for the ages
to rob me of my joy,
my hope—
but nope,
none of that at all.

Whenever I fall, you pick me back up again.
I'm so happy you stayed
and so grateful for what we've made.
Because of you, I'm provided a new world view
that shines a light into my darkness.
Thank you for staying.

-Stay

I don't need you to feel sane,
when it's plain that
you don't need me either.
And it's a shame
we couldn't keep it all together.
So much bad weather and storms,
it starts to feel like the norm.

But your hands kept mine warm.
But I don't think I can do this anymore.
I don't need you to feel sane,
though you keep running through my brain.
But I don't think you feel the same
and I've played that game too many times to count.
It always goes south.

I don't need to feel that way again.
So I meant it when I said
I don't need you.
Yet, I kept you around 'cause
I like the way your laugh sounds,
that cute smile when you make a joke,
and how you make me happy when I wanna mope.
I caught feels hard.

Now I don't know where those are.
The time we met feels so far away,
but I remember that day.
And now here I lay, trying to find a way to say
I just don't need you.
-I Don't Need You

I was doomed from the start,
this artist's heart
fell faster than a golden anchor in water.
Your saunter
and slight smile
drive me wild.

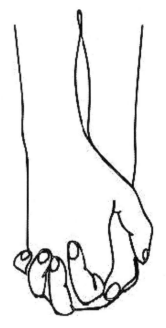

At first,
I was scared for how much I cared
for someone so new.

Like, could it be you?
Or am I just a creep? A weirdo?
Do I even belong here with you?
What did I do

to be so lucky to find someone like you?
I'm fascinated by who you are
and what you want to be,
on your own but also with me.
So you see, I love you.
Because you are you,
and I like me when I'm with you.
-I love you, sorry-

As the weather gets colder,
your light smolder melts into a grin
that look is a sin for how much joy it brings me.
Do ya kin,
my winter prince, that it be so cold outside,
yet we remain so warm?
A snowstorm you exchanged for the rain I'm used to.
I wait for your kisses
to remain on my lips
from you, winter prince
who slays all sadness with
a single bad joke,
who is kind to all common folk,
and treats love like no joke.
I can't wait to be with you,
winter prince,
to give you my kiss
and the touch
that we both crave so much.
See you soon, my winter prince.
Your kiss awaits.
-Winter Prince

Love Poem #3

You said you loved me in the fall, but as the air grew cold
and stole your warmth from me, your love went with it.
Now summer has come and you say
you were undone without me.
We will see how you feel about me when
I'm the cold one, and all is said and
done at the end of this summer heat,
and fall comes back again.

I can't help but love with all of me.
I don't know how else you see.
I will always love with all of me,
'cause love is part of me
and I want to share—
but some don't care for it.
I swore it was something everyone wanted,
but some don't know
how to care for it,

how to store it,
explore it,
adore it,
or know when it's good or
gone sour.

Some don't like to be showered in love.
Some get sick
and can't handle it.
I love with all of myself,
despite the risk.

To not get the kiss,
to be left and not be missed,
it's worth the risk,
'cause feeling unloved is something
I will never wish on anyone.
For without love, the world is undone,
so if I must remain unsung as a hero of love,

so be it,
but I will love with all of me
until the last sunset I see.
-I Love With All Of Me

There is a difference between loving someone and being in love with someone.
One can fall out of love with someone.
The warm sensation,
your most beautiful creation...
fleeting,

leaving nothing to cling to but feelings you once knew.
But when you love someone,
it doesn't matter what they look like,
what they do, because they knew something was different with you.

You see through the eye of their storm and build someplace warm
to brave their storm
together.

Cold winds can blow and be brisk to the bone,
but we remain steadfast.
Maybe we were built to last.

An agreement has passed
that through the magnificent vast of our existence we
remain persistent, resistant of harmful confrontations, have
healthy communications and never stop growing.
-In Love or Loving

I miss you even though we spoke yesterday.
I miss the way you caress my face and look at me like
time and space don't matter,
making all my worries scatter, and in that moment, I feel
like I matter.

I hope I don't shatter.

If you saw me tonight, you would ask, "What's the
matter?"
I'd say nothing,
and just hug you.
I just can't express
'cause I'm such a mess with how much I love you.
-*I Miss You*

Light rain
droplets stain the cement until it turns black.
Its scent fills the air as the wind blows without care.
But you're standing there with your hands in your pockets,
pretending to not be cold.

I offer my felt-lined pockets and you're sold—
as if it took much convincing.
It felt like something was missing,
without your touch.

Cold hands now warm wrapped in mine;
a chill goes down my spine,
so you pull me close.
The rain slows.

Your slight smile shows.
The cold tickles my nose.
That's when I know this night will change things.
'Cause the way you are looking at me is saying things
that I somehow understand.

I think we're vibing on this cold autumn night,
where the rain is light and I think I know who's taking me home
tonight.
-The Night I Knew

Dark Samurai Legend Epic Finale!

There once was a dark samurai.
He wore all black and had a scar over one eye. His travel companion was a
maiden with purple hair, stained with red from the demons they slayed.
Together they stayed for quite some time,
even when the world wasn't so divine.
Around the world they traveled to celebrate their connection,
never losing their affection.
From the seas of Europe
to the sands of the samurai's homeland,
they saw it all,
drank until they fell,
and danced even when there was no music at all,
ending every night with "I love you,"
meaning it even as each day came anew,
and becoming the people they always wanted to:
happy.

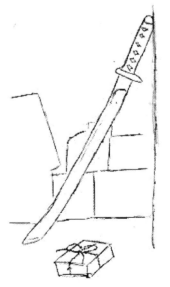

Chapter 3

Identity

My body is my avatar in the game of life.
If I got to choose,
I'd lose my boobs and wide hips.
Button downs and straight jeans would actually fit.

A slender build with muscle definition,
Not this curvy, fluffy rendition.
Trust me, the strength is there but all intimidation gets sucked from the
air as soon as I enter a room.
I am Thunder and Doom!
Fear me!
As soft awws leave my partner's mouth,
trust, without a doubt, things aren't always what they seem.

-I am not my body-

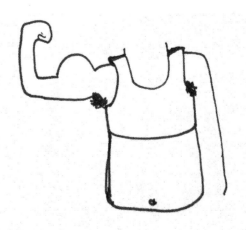

When I came out, I was sure,

without a doubt that

I was gonna get called out.

You're doing it wrong!

We've seen this song and dance and you are a cliché.

You can't be called they.

So I left myself out

of the conversation,

the whole non-binary categorization.

I didn't know how to identify.

I didn't want the words to come out like a lie.

So...

I did my research and searched

for the courage inside and talked

to my mom about it.

I doubted it would go very far.

Twenty-six and still learning who you are.

And like a Band-Aid, I let it rip and

she said,

"If you came here to tell me you identify as interesting, that's not news."

And in that moment, everything I knew had changed. What I thought

was being rearranged had just clicked into view. To my surprise,

everyone else already knew. I see the world from an interesting view.

"It's just something that's always been inside of you," she said.

Though news to me, it just felt nice to be seen.

-I Identify As Interesting

So if we're gonna be gay,
our wardrobe has to slay.
As if being queer came with a dress code.
Some unspoken trove...
behold! My gay clothes!
But...no.
So what do you do when the clothes you have don't fit you—
The new you? What do you do?
You grab your tribe, the people you vibe with, and fix it.
Rediscover yourself. It sometimes requires a little help.
I decided to go for comfort and not trendy, 'cause that can feel pretendy,
like wearing a costume.
But I wanted my wardrobe to express how complex
I can be while still having simplicity.
And you can't go wrong with the classics but...I make them my own.
So I have grown accustomed to my newest tough question:
what do I wear today?
The new dress or my new suspenders?
These extenders of how I slip in and out of genders help me find myself.
Logical, practical, comfortable—which outfit is all three?
Which one feels like me today?
Either way, I know I'll look good.
-Dress V. Suspenders

For some reason, the world is scared of different.
I think that's a manmade construct.
If one person can disrupt your whole way of life,
You must not get out very much.
Because the world is filled with so much beauty,
all it takes is one someone to make or break
a beautiful, different someone.
We must be better.
-*Different*

He/Her/ They/Them

I am a mystical orb of purple light in an
abandoned eighteenth-century home.
I am that feeling of joy when you buy a new crystal or stone.
When alone, I am a figure shrouded in darkness and mystery.
I am the witchery you feel on Halloween night,
personified.
I am an old soul.
I take pride in being people's console.
I am love and kindness and the definition
of brightness when I want to be.

I am a feeling, an experience of whatever I want to be.
I decided that for me.
A he, a her, a she, a him, a they/them.

What a mess, as I unload crumbs from my big chest pocket.
A pocket, a sack, useless mostly except for that.

A natural snack pack for popcorn, crumbs, or anything that manages to
fall down my shirt.
Sometimes...a place to keep money.
Apparently, they can be used to flirt but I never figured out that feature—
an iOS update my body didn't understand.

I just wanna shift from girl to man with ease.
But not with these...things in the way,
making button up shirts lay like I'm about to bust.

I wish I had a smaller bust. Trust, I would love it so much,
especially when I run.
But a binder is how I get the job done 'cause having big boobs isn't all
that fun.
That's as close to flat as I can get without getting rid of it.
If I did, where would I keep my phone?
-Flat Chest

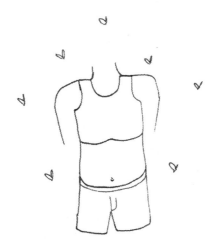

Skin—
something we live in, that some take pride in,
while others find themselves hidin'.
Skin—
also known as pigmentation,
which some use as a judgement call.
When did color make a person fall into a lesser category?
Purgatory:
where some fear to go.
Skin—
something that some are never comfortable in,
to fit on top of bodies they don't feel as their own,
then thrown to the wayside when they make a change to feel better.
What is better?
When the skin you're born in comes with complications,
who's smarter? Who must work harder or be slaughtered.

Skin.
It's supposed to be protection from the invasion of bacteria.
Sadly, opinions and judgment calls don't fall into that criteria.
This hysteria over surface area, though only
skin deep, is felt much deeper.

Skin.

Congratulations! You win. You made it into this
world with a full body to live in. Oh.
But watch out—your body may not fit in
to that cookie cutter idea that someone
cooked up and called beautiful.
They may have been truthful but that's just one view.
Let's see if you fit into something...else.

What else?
Skin—
the thin layer of tissue forming the natural
outer covering of the body of a person.
Who knew it could cause such a fuss?
-*Skin*

Is it a bird or a plane?
No, it's a man!
Does he have a long golden
mane or is it a short cut?
Shield or hammer?
I personally clamor over that one spider guy,
'cause in my eyes, he's taught me a
lot about doing the right thing,
despite everything,
no matter what obstacle,
that all things are possible with
hope in your arsenal.

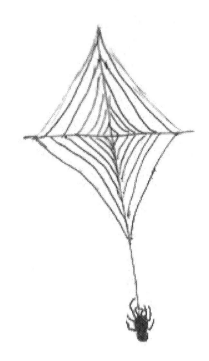

Heroes, real or fictitious, keep us ambitious,
striving for better, giving us
something to look up to,
though being super isn't all
it's cracked up to be.
It comes with great responsibility.
It helps if you're kind, of sound
mind, and know your appearance
is not how you're defined.
It's not always about who's the bad guy, but
where your morals lie being super or not.
Those strong women and men give
me the confidence to try again,
to be my own superhero.
-Superheroes

Backward, forward, onward, upward—
all directions with no clear destination.

Keep moving forward they say,
moving through the motions of our day to day.
But I gotta say, that's a lot of movement with no sign of
improvement or promise for better.

Some of us have forgotten where we started.
Our new selves and past ideals have parted.
So we look back,
but looking and moving are two different things.

Backward is forgetting what you've learned,
being so concerned with the things you can't control and
you fold back into yourself like origami.

But looking back is seeing how far you've come,
all the lessons you've learned from and the shiny new
person you've become.

Love your past self unconditionally,
and don't punish yourself for the things you had yet to
learn,
and somehow that will help.
Look back with love, but there is no moving backward,
just moving on.
-*Backwards*

Enough

What is enough?
I have struggled my whole life on whether I
was the answer to that question.

Am I enough for my mother?
Am I enough for my father?
Am I enough to get the things I want?
Am I enough for anything?
History shows that my existence has been at the admittance
of a man—usually a white man, but not limited to...
like I am limited to the right to make choices with my own body.

My body is not my own.
I am owned by whoever marries me,
for without marriage I have no value.
Those are the values of a time that was not so sublime.
I'm happy I was not around to see the sunshine on a world like that.

I wouldn't know how to act.
Burned at the stake and shot on sight
to have the sheer might to know they weren't right.
I am alive—therefore I am enough.
No one taught me that.

There are no stats or facts,
simply the act of being makes that a fact.
Yet the act of making people feel inferior is a fad that refuses to die.

Some people lay in bed at night wishing they
could just fly to someplace new,
where the people don't know the old you,
to start anew and just be enough for yourself.
When will it be enough?

When children die?
When bodies lie in the streets?
What then?
When will we look at one another and see we are the same?
That I do not know.
But I'm here writing this poem to show
something you need to know...
You are enough
For just being who you are.

Don't let any fad, Chad, or iron clad man tell you different.
You exist.
That makes you enough.
Now go make a difference.

According to my TV and other media,
I don't exist—
not simply missed,
ignored,
an eyesore,
a smudge on the complexion
of a perception of our world.

Black, queer, and no fear of being myself:
my sister thought it was a cry for help.
It's just a phase.
You'll be amazed...it was not.
I know what I'm not.

I do exist but the mainstream media refuses this.
With no representation, my own nation and most of the world thinks my mere
existence is not the norm.
So there is this push to conform aggressively to someone else's norm.

I simply won't have that.
If you're mad at that,
it's your problem,
because I do exist
and I'll be damned
you don't know this.
-I Don't Exist

People are like French fries.
some are straight,
some are waffles,
some are crinkle cut,
but some come out like me:
golden brown, seasoned, and curly.
-Fries

There are black people out there who like me.
You see for a long time I truly
disliked the people I looked like.
They never had anything nice to say to me.
So I would flee the scene,
to the whitest people I could find
who would like me for me.

They would just be so mean
for just being me.
You talk like a white girl.
You are such an Oreo.
You aren't black. You can't be.
Your skin and that smile are just an act.
It's a fact, bitch—you ain't black.

But the mirror says otherwise.
I have nothing to hide.
I'm not a lie.
I'm just that happy to be alive.
All. The. Time.
I'm older now.
Those words still sting.

I have moved through that,
grew through that,
flew through that and became the person I wanted to be.
And then I found people like me, *who like me!*
Who look like me!

They really like me,

'cause for so long I didn't think they did.
So the Oreo kid found a place to fit in.
Funny enough, my friends don't really care about the color of my skin.

Because they love what's within.
My skin is *not* a label
for how I should be loved,
hugged, or to whom I make love,
or if I use drugs,
have good lungs,
or play ball.
Forget it all.

I am whatever I decide to be—

and I just want to be me.
-Black People Like Me

Chapter 4

Sexy Stuff

Wake up, go to work, and come home,
back from the vanilla zone:

a cone of isolation where the organizations hold all the
control.
You hold your eye roll.

Working hard takes a toll
on your heart and soul but not your sex drive.
I can't wait to get a hold of you when I get home again.

A space where my wicked
deeds won't be condemned.
Where my sadistic side can roam and stretch,
as I place a firm grip around your neck.

You moan and I'm taken,
but not mistaken
that you are shaken with lust.
Trust I'll take care
of all of that 'til you bust.
Trust when I'm in charge,
I'll take care of that lust.
-The One in Charge

They gazed at my naked body, laced in darkness—
their darkness—it envelops me.
I can't see as my body adores their cool,
gentle touch.
It's almost too much
when they grab my throat from behind.
Where's my mind
as their fingers glide
down the curve of my waist?

Their embrace—all I want is a taste of them.
Oh to taste them on my lips.
Please...just one kiss?

Your lips,
that's what I miss—your soft kiss.
I try to resist your tight grip
but your strength persists
and gets tighter.

I feel lighter
as a soft moan escapes my mouth.
Their fingers heading south.
Their hand over my mouth
as I writhe with pleasure.
I hear a whisper in my ear:
"You're my special treasure and there's nothing you can do about it."
And before I knew it, I was pinned against a wall,
their hand on my neck again
and their lips exploring mine again.
I can't protest that this is a test
and I'm failing.

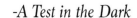

"Be still," they said "or I win."
Falling under their spell again.
They can tell,
as their darkness builds into a menacing grin;
it's absolute sin.
I don't want it to end.
They win.
I failed my test...but we had the best sex.

-A Test in the Dark

Humans need touch.
It's what fills us with lust and brings such a rush.
To touch,
To feel and understand what's real—
it's something we need
to feed and nurture the seed that is our souls.
'Cause no matter how strong we are at night,
when the rest of the world is far, we feel our scars.
Some wounds still bleed though the blood is unseen.
But the universe is keen
and sometimes makes the perfect
scene for play.
Foreplay,
touchdown,
or score—
all words to describe this fuss.

Trust, everyone has nights when
the bed feels cold from the lack of another soul to...
touch touch touch,
steal and call their own.
Their warmth melts away your sorrows of loneliness and worldly pain—
nothing to lose but all to gain.
One night stands become lands and grounds for foundations that can last a lifetime
or just the night.
The goodbyes are never happy,
usually never sappy.
But there is no denying that their touch helped,
fulfilled your lust,
gave you their trust,
and now, no rust or dust on your tired heart.
Just enough cleaning to keep everything streaming and flowing
so you can keep going,
never showing those scars the light of day.
And the lust for touch is tamed for now.

-Touch

So this is what it feels like to get the guy you want:
no fuss,
no rush,
nothing but lust. A craving?
So that is it.
Never quite believe it would happen.
So suddenly with no warning, but I thought I knew.
I just didn't think it would happen so soon,
no time to swoon or set the mood.
We had one candle that warmed the night,
a gift I gave with pure delight, in hopes that the light my candle brought would fill my
broken heart with someone else's happiness.

Yet, there I was, lying there,
fair,
bare,
and a little scared.
I had fun. I didn't want to run.
Set my phaser to stun and we went off like a gun,
and now it's...
done.
I watch the sunrise and to my surprise, the world is still. I'm not ill. I feel content, not spent
that I went there, to his lair, with little care of what our actions might lead to.

Now.
Wow. I'm sitting here and I strangely feel clear.
Sheer crystal, refracting my future lonely nights to day.
I think I need to go drink a glass of wine...alone.
Don't need to call anyone on the phone.
I'm not made of stone, just tougher to crack, lacking in fear of being alone with him on a
whim by myself.
It helped,
lifted a weight off my shoulders.
Loads and loads of boulders...gone.
Doesn't feel like anything is wrong.
My feelings for you just...gone.

-Interesting

Looking left,
looking right—
your chest feels tight as a faraway beast stalks in the night,
just out of sight,
waiting, anticipating the hunt, the kill to get its prey.
But what happens to those too foolish to seek out the beast?
The few are fascinated by the beast's sharp claws and teeth it has to spare,
making the hunt slightly unfair,
but the ones who seek it don't care.
Tension hangs in the air, as you walk into the beast's lair.
You find it and all you can do is stare at its beauty.
You see, the beast can recognize your demons inside with the darkness in your eyes.
Both of you are mesmerized by each other's looks.
How one so tough and scary could be so soft.
How one could be so fair and fragile and also be so cracked and unspackled.
As you both step closer, the tension melts with everything else.
You and the beast feast on each other's gaze.
All alone, but together,
now inches away.
What used to hide in the shadows now strokes your hair and caresses your cheek.
How are you capable of being so sweet?
Then you remember why you did this chase: to literally face the beast
that dwells in the dark, so it doesn't feel alone. To be alone together.
They both dealt with their own demons forever tethered.
-The Monster Inside

Chapter 5

People and Places

Beautiful places, gorgeous spaces,
are the places we go to relax,
detach, yet find contact with ourselves,
look at seashells and explore where
creatures dwell.

You must crawl out of your shell and find
something new,
someone new.
But who?
Don't worry, your heart knew.
It's who you came with or came to.
'Cause it's better not to travel alone,
'cause talking on the phone is not the same.
Beautiful places can seem lame to some extent.
No one to show that cool thing you found
in the road or share that beautiful sunset
that showed nearly all the colors of the rainbow.

Someone once said it doesn't matter where you go, but who
you're with, and now I'm starting to see how that makes
sense.
-Beautiful places

Beautiful Moment #2

The breeze is brisk as I step out.
The air is cold as others shout and get used to it,
move through it.
I don't know how they do it, but they manage.
My breath makes clouds around my head, as I
wish to be warm by my heater instead,
maybe even in bed, but the crisp air as it whips
through my hair, I stare into the distance.
Feel the cold on my skin but am filled to the brim with joy as
I see children play with their scarves around their necks.
A man walks by wearing sandals...what the heck?
California in the winter is a sight to see.

A Series of Unfortunate Nights #2

Sore. Countless shifts a complete bore, but the past few have left me sore. Standing up for hours on end, as I pretend my feet don't ache from lack of shoe support. My view distorts on things as countless people tell me how to do my job. This slob in front of me with a crooked eye complains of his utter waste of time, as I just want him and others like him to get out of my face. The sheer pace of these shifts drifts from crazed to slow. My exhaustion is beginning to show. Only three more hours to go. You can do this. Put up with this. But this pain...is beginning to gnaw at my brain as the one hundredth person asks me a question I answered only seconds beforehand. Yet there I stand repeating myself for the idiot in front of me. You see a perky, even quirky young girl with a smile like no other, but if you heard of the things that some people have said, you'd wonder how I still stand. Sore, slightly poor, just sore with bruises you can't see. You can't help me, 'cause I'm there to help you find your seat so you can eat at a dirty table I wiped down myself that no one swept under as cold French fries rest where your feet are set. But that's not my fault. And the result is soreness.

Beautiful Moment #1

I look in awe at the giant buildings, wet from the light rain. No pain, just pavement stains. This feeling in the air, it isn't fair. Why don't I feel this way at home? The skyscrapers turn to brownstones. Businesses turn into homes and I'm in a new place. I feel safe, in this nice place. No time to waste; I must explore everything! The light shines through my fingers. The smell of roasted peanuts lingers. The parks here are even nicer! Food's a little pricier. I wanna stay here, maybe live. Back to the brownstones. I'm alone in my own little lair. Now this is my space that I don't have to share, but I'm willing. I am basement sitting. This place, the pace, is just the way I like it. I just can't shake it; there is no mistaking it. New York, New York, how I miss it. I would really like to revisit. The people, my family there, and all the stories they must want to share. I wish them well in the cold winters there. I wish them all the joys the world has to offer, as long as the snow isn't the stopper. So let me end this proper. With so much love, I must bid you adieu.
Je t'aime mon du New York.

The room is packed,
stacked with people and food.
Don't be rude; say hi—
hi and bye.
Sigh.
On to the next one.
Maybe this one will be fun?
This person could be your sun
to this dark and gloomy party.
Hi and bye.
A little part of you dies
as you check the time.
It's only been an hour
and this party has already gone sour.
Can I go home?
Maybe I'll roam the open parts of this venue,
see what's on the menu of this person's life,
if the venue is a house.
Where's the bathroom?
Let my phone become a vacuum
to suck me out of this situation.
This celebration has left me
with the sensation of
being alone in a crowded room,
where it's safe to assume
I'd feel better being actually alone.
-Alone in A Crowded Room

No. (A Complete Sentence)
I said no.
No.
As in:
N. O.
I executed my right to have boundaries
because I don't have boundless seas of energy
and I refuse to let lethargy be my way of life,
So I'm done.
Your argument is done
'cause there is none
because *no* is a complete sentence.

Pretty face with nothing behind it,
hiding the stupid
behind a mask
that can't seem to hold conversation.
The sensation to connect without sex,
use common sense
and enjoy someone's presence,
their vibe,
not just someone to ride
into their empty headed sunset.

It makes me upset,
how someone having a pretty face
can misplace so many minds,
making their thoughts
as deep as a kiddie pool.

As many girls like myself
drool over their nice bodies,
we settle for these atrocities
of common sense
and the huge lack of it.

I quit.
Looking at someone
and think they're the one without having a conversation,
has my generation sadly mistaken with what being with someone should be like.

You have similar likes and passions for things,
if not each other.
Being together should give you wings,
make you want to sing and dance,
even if you can't.

It's not something you can land
by clicking on pictures and just hope
he will be your future mister.
It's almost sinister the lack of connecting
we do when trying to reach out,
speak out,
scream and shout, "Please do!

instead of writing in all caps
and misspelling "you're."
The internet was invented to connect people to all the knowledge they seek.
Somehow we hit our peak, then fell down somewhere,
and that gives girls like me a headache.
Heart aches because people can be fake, making me cry, "For God's sake!"

How can people so stupid exist?
Was there something that I missed?
There is no excuse for it.
If you have a pretty face, that shouldn't mean that you get a pass to not be able to last
in a ten minute conversation.
All I ask is for that sweet sensation to connect without sex and not have it be so
complex.
Do you get me?
-Pretty Face

There's something I used to do,
abused to do,
something I refuse to do,
something I used to be.
But I could see that I needed to vent
without consent—
just let it out,

Scream

Shout

Just to break my silence.

Reliant on the sounds and the grounds to make a point,
joint thoughts and connections when we make recollections of past burns and jokes.

I yearn to feel smart,
as sharp as a dart with how on point I am.
But it can't be helped; I did it to myself,
since I can't stand the company of the stupid.
Unintelligent?
Unwise?
Mentally displaced?
You catch my drift.

My mind has spent so much time pressing record and rewind on all the times I've felt
dumb and missed a line—
just not in time.

If I had a dime for every time that's happened...
maybe you'd see a goofball like me
on TV and you can't help but watch.

Start

Stop

Rewind

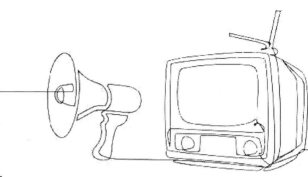

Gonna need a mop for things
I should've stopped and not said,
what should've stayed in my head.
It seems like everything I say goes south.

I'm starting to doubt my words
and the things I've seen.
I don't even know what I sometimes mean.

So I make rhymes in times where I feel small in size, which helps bring everything
back into view.
I am smart and my brain won't fart when it really matters.
My head has gotten better
with rhyming,

Timing
Compartmentalizing
Rationalizing
Speaking out
Being loud
And not being too proud
Or knowing when I don't want to be around.
So silent, I will never be again.
-Silent

The world is war and all the obstacles
we face are all the battles
that bring us closer to winning.
I found a unit,
a couple of young fighters,
who I thought could take me
where I wanted to go.
I was wrong.
In times when I needed boosting,
all I felt was the cold stings
of put downs.
I was getting pummeled
by explosions of emotions.
The blasts blew out my hearing
and made me blind
to how I let people mistreat me.

But *now...*

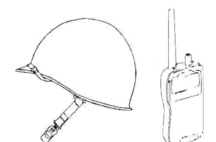

the final bits of dust have fallen
and the skies have cleared.
I have moved past my fears, tears,
and disappeared from their radar.
My strategizing and timing have gotten faster,
and now I'm a master.
My ideas are priceless to sell.
I don't have a tell.
I strike without a sign.
And as I move forward, I find more of my kind to run with.
Through the woods like a pack of wolves ready to attack.
I am raw power that can shower you with praise if you give our mission your best
shot.
But I look to my sides, forward, and realize
I got my own six and I don't need anyone to watch it.
-*Watching My Own Six*

Inconsequential

What makes an act or fact inconsequential?
Did the words come from someone not essential?
At least not to you.
Were their intentions clear or see through?

Let's look at the facts of any act.
Science, if you will, that any action has an equal or greater reaction.
So who decides what fraction of information of a conversation is
inconsequential?
Isn't all information essential?
Real or fake?
What if lives are at stake?
What if your fate lies in wait while someone else decides if you're
essential to their end goal?

Somehow we forgot that in every human lies a soul.
Their end goal may be to just go home on this plane or the next.
But I cannot stress enough
how, when overlooked, information could save nations of people from
strife.
When it's not just your life,
nothing is inconsequential.

Today I created a new world.
It was crazy how it uncurled and unraveled.
Traveled to places I never thought of before,
as if it were stored somewhere in my brain—
no pain,

maybe a little insane
but not lame!
Maybe it will bring me fame?
My and all my friends' names up in lights,
with awesome fights,
frights,
beautiful sights and more for all to adore.

It's something I can't wait to explore and see more
when it's not on paper.
This old world had only been a caper of my time.
I whine, dine, take a nap, and chime back in when I'm needed.
My head starts to spin with all the stories I have to tell and yell from mountaintops.

But my heart stops,
my pen drops—
I'm lost.

It's not ready, unsteady, let's rip it, shred it, make it confetti.
Is this world ready to see this new world I've created and stated as my own?

Will it show that I've grown from my mistakes?
Without haste, let's get it in front of someone's face,
but I don't want to waste anyone's time.
I'm making this rhyme to show
where I'm coming from,
what I've done,
the mental battles I've won

so my new world doesn't get shunned.
It's beautiful to me and want the whole world to see
for a small fee (to keep the lights on),
but I want them to see my passion has not faded and I'm not jaded from past obstacles.

Sit back, relax, and enjoy the show of my world.

That I have known and grown to love,
with characters that shine like the stars above.

So don't shove my world aside,
'cause I have died a thousand time to make it,
I can't shake it,
The feeling of letting it be seen.
But it must be fresh, clean, and sharp.
So I gotta be smart;
It is my art.

Can't blow my one chance to make audiences dance with how awesome my world is.
So I must be patient,
for all the time I've spent and just remember to
never quit.
-Creating a World

Gone

A human life doesn't last very long.
They can be laughing one day and the next be gone.
Gone.
No more laughs or gasps or so on.
Just gone.
You ponder and wonder where did you go wrong?
What could I have done
to help someone be here just a little bit longer?
Maybe if I was stronger?
But the "what ifs" will kill me too,
wondering what else I could do,
to be there for you or just say goodbye.
Just know you are loved and the time we spent together
that strengthened our bond, lives on.
Since you've moved on,
I will in time.
Your kind heart will live on in mine.
Though you have passed on,
you will never truly be gone.

Aren't you over that already?
That was ages ago—come on.
Come on, forget how you wronged me,
so you can do it again?
The transgression
a lesson you forced me to learn
that you now want me to forget.
I'm over it,
The mist has cleared,
and I see you.

Sure I'll tell you all is forgiven,
so smitten with the idea
of you having the opportunity to let me down—
again.

The original sin
that you seem to bask in
led me in to trust you.
Must you make a big deal of my hesitation?
'Cause that sensation makes me feel crazy
for feeling anything at all.

Ahh the gall!
Here I am
in a bathroom stall
crying,
Trying to figure out how I got here again.
But I'm over it.
Just haven't forgotten.
-Over It

-What's up with you?-
Do I gotta solve another mystery?
I see you looking blue;
I don't know what to do?

What's up with you?
The trail leads back to this afternoon.
I wanna help you feel better soon.
So I'm gonna solve this mystery.

If I make you laugh,
will you give me a clue of
what's up with you?

'Cause you being sad will simply not do,
especially when I'm hanging out with you.
All right—
stay locked down.

I'll be here when you come around,
but I'm not down to let you mope about it.
Don't doubt it, just to help you not think about it
and go back to having fun.

So when we're done
and I get one smile out of you,
you won't have to deal with whatever it is alone—
unless you want to.

What is a fantasy?

Things in our minds we make up and see?

Are they dreams and hopes we pray might be?

Or is fantasy romanticized reality?

Something we use to flee from our problems and sorrows

just to make it to our tomorrows.

Reality can be the dream

where we scheme and make memes that everyone can relate to,

maybe meet someone new in this reality.

Ha, a fallacy making fantasy into reality.

That's the limiting thoughts of some.

But you can become anyone when you control your reality,

complete with a new personality,

be anything you want

because we create our own reality.

-Real World V. Fantasy

Everything is opening up again.
The masses flood in as if
we didn't *just* have a plague,
a plague whose destruction destroyed our reality.
My whole mentality has changed.

I don't feel the same.

Life isn't just some game I can win.
It's filled with sin,
hate, and greed that no one can satiate.

I've lost my appetite

because the world I love isn't all full of light but...
darkness.

As the world opens back up again,
I have been awakened to the darkness
that resides here, but I won't live in fear.

For everything I hold dear requires
me to shift through this unclear time and...go outside.
As I come out of my hole,
A whole year—gone.
I struggle to find a grip on the world I once knew.
What do I miss about you?

Coffee shops
Chats with kind strangers

No feelings of immediate danger after touching my face.
I'm trying to make a case for this old world but it can't exist.
I'm not the same Miss I used to be.
I'm a they/them that refuses to be put down,

knocked down,

or given the runaround.

My patience for the past tense of this world is slim to none.

I'm done with past ideals and letting others' emotional wheels run all over me.

I will remain steadfast with my new boundaries.

Talk less.

Listen more.

As the world I once adored changes to something new,

I will pave a path for something to look forward to.

So if they don't like the new us

that has emerged from the ashes and dust,

they can kiss our asses.

Life can be hard, but we are tougher now.

Somehow I don't think that's a bad thing.

So out into the world we go.

-*Out Into The World*

I'm starting to understand how our plans are going...

I don't think I can hang out with you.

The way you do you is not the way I do me.

You see, we have planned this day a week in advance.

It's like a well-choreographed dance where we always seem to miss each other.

But at last!

We hook up,

link up,

but not sync up.

You made two phone calls and answered another one.

How fun

to get to hang out with you while you're on the phone with someone.

After the fifth time, you check your phone.

I'm done.

The phone won.

Clearly my time is not as valuable as yours.

You have successfully made me feel like a bore,

a chore you didn't want to get done, but had to.

If you only knew how much my time with you mattered to me. Then you would see

that I long for those moments for us to laugh and sing with glee,

but sadly you're not like that with me.

I wish that's how it could be.

-I Don't Think I Can Hang Out With You

Rough, callused, hardened skin,
scarred from all the heartache you've been in.
Layers upon layers you've built up of this damaged skin.
You fear to let anyone in.
Relationships are great, but you don't want to go through it all again.
Alone again,
so you stay in,
stay home—
at least here you choose to be alone.
If you get lonely, call someone on the phone,
'cause lonely and alone are two separate things,
but one is really hard to shake when it takes hold.
You run a hand over your newest scar.
It's hard to let people know who you are,
but some people really dig scars.
Just saying.

Thank you for reading my book.
I hope the thoughts I wrote in loneliness
made you feel less alone.
-*Damaged Skin*

Thank you for reading my book. I hope the thoughts I
wrote in loneliness made you feel less alone.

Acknowledgments

A special thanks to the following people and institutions:

Casey Suddeth
Tiffany Daniel -Jones
Cinnamon Aldridge
James Rhaburn
Vince Elra
Madi
The Painted Brain
Archway Publishing
My family

Without all of your love and support, this book wouldn't have happened.

Instagram: Nikkislife123_
nicolejulian.com

About the Author

Nicole Rose Julian grew up in Culver City, California, where they took their first college-level screenwriting class at the age of 12. They haven't stopped writing since. They attended acting and film classes at the American Musical & Dramatic Academy and the New York Film Academy in Hollywood, California. After finding more success in their art they made it their full-time job. With lots of love and support from family and friends, The Relatable Poetry Journal was encouraged to see the light of day. Nicole now has made it their personal mission to inspire people to live as their most authentic selves through their craft, while supporting causes geared towards mental health and wellness.

Printed in the United States
by Baker & Taylor Publisher Services